I0803372

STRENGTH IN NUMBERS: ANIMAL GROUPS

BIRD GROUPS

BY CLARA MacCARALD

Core Library
An Imprint of Abdo Publishing
abdobooks.com

Cover Image: Blue-and-gold macaws form both large and small flocks. They roost in family groups.

abdobooks.com

Published by Abdo Publishing, a division of ABDO, PO Box 398166, Minneapolis, Minnesota 55439.

Core Library™ is a trademark and logo of Abdo Publishing.

Printed in the United States of America, North Mankato, Minnesota.
052025
092025

THIS BOOK CONTAINS RECYCLED MATERIALS

Cover Photo: Shutterstock Images
Interior Photos: Luke Dray/Getty Images News/Getty Images, 4–5; Louis Lotter Photography/Shutterstock Images, 6, 43; Vic Thornley/Shutterstock Images, 10–11; Red Line Editorial, 13; Whittaker Wildlife UK/Alamy, 14; Tony Mills/Shutterstock Images, 15; Steve Byland/Shutterstock Images, 18–19, 45; Lee Dalton/Alamy, 21; Humberto Olarte Cupas/Alamy, 22; Bill Coster/Alamy, 25; Elliotte Rusty Harold/Shutterstock Images, 26–27; Karen Hogan/Shutterstock Images, 29; Danita Delimont/Shutterstock Images, 30; Karel Bock/Shutterstock Images, 32; Ivan Hoermann/Shutterstock Images, 34–35; Shutterstock Images, 37 (penguin), 37 (phytoplankton, krill), 37 (fish, squid, mammals); Thomas Barrat/Shutterstock Images, 38; Nick Rule/Alamy, 40

Editor: Laura Stickney
Series Designer: Ryan Gale

Library of Congress Control Number: 2024948985

Publisher's Cataloging-in-Publication Data

Names: MacCarald, Clara, author.
Title: Bird groups / by Clara MacCarald
Description: Minneapolis, Minnesota: Abdo Publishing, 2026 | Series: Strength in numbers: animal groups | Includes online resources and index.
Identifiers: ISBN 9781098297251 (lib. bdg.) | ISBN 9798384919773 (ebook)
Subjects: LCSH: Birds--Juvenile literature. | Bird communities--Juvenile literature. | Animal colonies--Juvenile literature. | Birds--Behavior--Juvenile literature.
Classification: DDC 598.2--dc23

CONTENTS

CHAPTER ONE

FLOCKING FOR SAFETY

The African grassland swarms with thousands of small birds. They are red-billed queleas. Some stand on the ground, plucking seeds from the grass. Others rise up like a cloud. The flock moves in a pattern. Birds in the front land on the ground, while birds in the back fly over them and land ahead of them. As birds in the back eat all the seeds around them, they fly toward the front. The flock advances in a rolling wave. This helps the birds find almost all the seeds in their path.

Red-billed queleas are one of the world's most abundant bird species. They form large flocks in order to feed on grass seeds or grains.

Red-billed queleas have reddish, cone-shaped bills and light-brown feathers. They often perch close together in trees near water holes or feeding areas.

The sun bakes the hot landscape. Without water, the queleas could not survive in this dry land. Soon the birds will need to drink. But water holes are risky places to visit. Predators can hide in or near the water. To stay safe, the queleas must work together. The flock billows up from the ground like smoke. Queleas in other flocks see the group. They follow it, rising off the grassland. The cloud of birds streams toward a nearby water hole.

A lanner falcon perches in the bushes by the water. It is waiting for prey. The quelea flock arrives, swooping into a tree that hangs over the water. Queleas crowd onto the branches. Some birds perch on plants that have drooped down onto the water's surface. The birds begin to drink. The falcon sees its chance. It launches into the air. But queleas in the tree spot the predator coming. They sound the alarm. Soon the whole flock sweeps back into the safety of the tree's branches. The falcon soars away.

Queleas spend their lives in flocks. Some flocks have more than a million birds. Living in large numbers helps queleas survive.

COOPERATIVE FALCONS

Lanner falcons live in Africa, Europe, and Asia. A pair of bonded lanner falcons often cooperates while hunting. One falcon may fly ahead of the other to scare small birds out of cover. This makes the birds fly into the open. Then the second falcon swoops in for the kill. Hunting together helps lanner falcons catch more prey than they would while hunting alone. The pair also cooperates to raise chicks. When falcon chicks grow older, they join the hunt. The adults help the young falcons get meals. The youngsters learn hunting skills from their parents too.

BIRDS BY THE NUMBERS

Like queleas, many birds find strength in numbers. Birds are endothermic vertebrates that grow feathers. All birds have wings, but some species have lost the ability to fly. All bird species lay eggs too. Birds live on every continent on Earth.

While some birds live alone or in pairs, many benefit from living in groups. Parents and their offspring may stay together in family groups. Other times, unrelated birds flock together. Some species even join flocks that contain several other

V FLIGHT

Flocks of large birds such as geese often form V shapes in the sky. The geese do not have to use as much energy to fly when flying in this shape. Birds in the front of the V move the air with their wingbeats. The moving air helps lift the birds behind them. This means birds flying behind the leader don't have to work as hard. As the birds in front get tired, they fall back and let others take the lead. Flying in a V rather than in a straight line also helps each bird keep an eye on its neighbors. Paying attention helps the geese stay together.

bird species. Birds may nest in colonies too. Many species migrate together or spend the winter in groups, even if they live alone during the rest of the year.

Birds live in flocks for many reasons. They may gather for safety. In a group, there are more eyes to watch out for predators. Each group member has a smaller chance of being eaten than a bird living alone does. Group members can also learn things from each other, such as where to migrate or nest. They may learn how to find food. Some birds cooperate to get meals. Living in large numbers helps many birds survive and reproduce.

EXPLORE ONLINE

Chapter One talks about how birds form groups. As you know, every source is different. What information does the website below give about birds? How is the information from the website the same as the information in Chapter One? What new information did you learn from the website?

BIRD

abdocorelibrary.com/bird-groups

CHAPTER TWO

EUROPEAN STARLINGS

The European starling is a very common bird. More than a billion starlings live around the world. These birds form huge flocks that can number more than a million individuals. European starlings are native to Europe, Asia, and northern Africa. In the 1800s, humans introduced starlings to new regions because they hoped the birds would control insect pests on farms. The species now lives in the Americas and Australia.

European starlings have dark, iridescent feathers that change color depending on the season. Starling flocks are known for being very noisy.

FLOCKS IN NEW PLACES

In the past, people brought many bird species to new places around the world. House sparrows were native to Europe, Asia, and Africa before humans introduced them elsewhere. Today, flocks of house sparrows live around houses and farmland on every continent except Antarctica. People once brought rock pigeons to new places too. They wanted to use the birds as a food source and as message carriers. Today, these pigeons live in cities and natural areas worldwide. The common myna is native to Asia. People keep mynas as pets, but some escape. Mynas now live in North America, Africa, and Australia. They can also be found on many islands.

Starlings eat many kinds of insects, fruits, and seeds. The birds nest in cavities. These holes can be in trees, buildings, or nest boxes.

Starlings thrive in many habitats. Some live among humans, taking advantage of man-made food sources such as garbage. Starlings sometimes take fruit from orchards or feed at bird feeders. They may attack and drive off other birds at feeders.

EUROPEAN STARLINGS AROUND THE WORLD

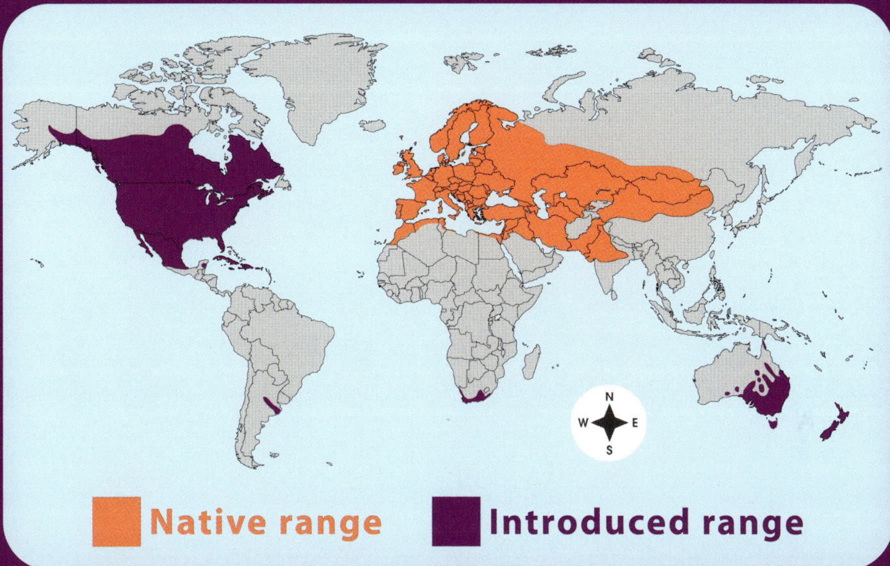

This map shows the native range of European starlings, or where they originally lived before the 1800s. It also shows starlings' introduced range, or where they spread after people brought them to new places. What do you notice about these two ranges? Why do you think starlings spread to some places but not others?

ROOSTS AND MURMURATIONS

For most of the year, starlings spend the night in groups called roosts. Starling roosts form in towns and cities. They may also form in forests, in wetlands, and on farms. Some starlings perch on trees. Some perch on

Starlings often roost on structures that have ledges, holes, or sheltered nooks. Flocks have been seen roosting on bridges, skyscrapers, and office buildings.

buildings or other man-made structures. When large numbers of birds roost together, it can help individual birds stay safe from predators. During the day, starlings usually leave the roost to feed.

In fall and winter, roosts can include millions of birds. Starlings form smaller flocks in the spring and summer. These flocks sometimes contain other kinds of birds too. During the breeding season, red-winged blackbirds nest in small groups. But in winter, they form large flocks with starlings and other birds. Species in these flocks include common grackles, brown-headed cowbirds, and American robins.

Starling murmurations usually take place at sundown during the winter months. They form in the sky over a flock's roosting site.

As night approaches, starlings head back toward their roost. They gather nearby. Right before sunset, many starlings rise into the air and form huge cloudlike formations that constantly change shape. These are called murmurations. Scientists aren't sure exactly why murmurations happen before roosting. The display may advertise a roost so more birds join it. The more birds in a roost, the more body heat to warm the group. But the display may also help starlings look out for danger.

When a predator such as a falcon attacks, the murmuration responds. It changes shape as the starlings flee the threat. The birds may bunch together or spread out. Each bird watches about seven of its closest neighbors to decide where to move. Change happens quickly as movements ripple out over the entire flock. This confuses the predator, making it difficult for it to focus on a single bird. The murmuration ends with the starlings entering the roost all at once. They spend the night there, relying on the safety of numbers.

BIRD MOB

Starlings don't always flee predators. Sometimes they fight back. Mobbing is when several small birds go after a larger bird or mammal. The mobbing group may contain several species working together. The small birds might swoop or dive at the predator. They make a lot of noise, which attracts more birds to the mob. A predator has a hard time hunting when it can't surprise its prey. So when a predator faces a mob, it gives up and goes away.

STRAIGHT TO THE SOURCE

Danish photographer Søren Solkær traveled across Europe taking pictures of starling murmurations, which he shared in a book. In a 2022 article, he explained the thought process behind his work:

In creating this series of images, I was inspired by a number of other art forms, including classical landscape painting, calligraphy, and Japanese woodblock prints. I was also inspired by the birds themselves.

When starlings move as a single unified organism and assert themselves against the sky, they create a strong visual expression, like that of a calligraphic brush stroke. Lines and shapes emerge within the swarm, bringing to life physical abstractions and calling to mind the patterns formed by interfering waves.

Source: Søren Solkær. "Gazing at the 'Black Sun': The Transfixing Beauty of Starling Murmurations." *New York Times*, 4 Apr. 2022, nytimes.com. Accessed 28 Oct. 2024.

CONSIDER YOUR AUDIENCE

Adapt this passage for a different audience, such as your principal or friends. Write a blog post conveying this same information for the new audience. How does your post differ from the original text and why?

CHAPTER THREE

BLACK VULTURES

Black vultures are large birds with a wingspan of about 5 feet (1.5 m). They are social birds that forage, feed, and rest together. Sometimes hundreds of black vultures gather in roosts. These roosts may also include turkey vultures, a related species. Black vultures live in southern North America and throughout Central and South America. Some populations migrate or travel short distances to avoid winter weather. Black vultures mostly eat carrion,

Black vultures have dark feathers and bare heads. Mating pairs stay together for life and develop close-knit family groups.

RAPTOR MIGRATION

Many raptor species flock during migration, even if they don't live together during the rest of the year. Raptor flocks can include thousands of individuals. Raptors migrate together because land features, such as large bodies of water or tall mountains, force birds to follow specific routes across the continents. There are several major raptor migration routes around the world. The migrating raptors take advantage of places where air naturally rises. This helps the birds catch a lift for long distances. Moving in a flock can help raptors find these rising air currents.

or dead animals. But they also eat other things, such as eggs and rotting plants. Sometimes they kill and eat small animals.

Black vultures rely on their eyesight to find food, so they spend much of their time soaring above fields and woodlands looking for carrion. They rest and nest in forested areas. They also nest in abandoned buildings and on skyscrapers. Black vultures often thrive around human settlements, where they feed on garbage and on animals that have

Black vultures sometimes gather near bodies of water to eat dead fish that wash up along the shore.

been hit by cars. People usually call a group of vultures a committee. But a flock of vultures in the air is called a kettle. A group feeding on a carcass is known as a wake.

A VULTURE'S SOCIAL LIFE

Black vulture roosts are places where birds can rest for the night and interact with each other. Parents continue to feed their young for months after they leave the nest. When parents and their offspring meet at a roost, the

Black vulture chicks are born with brownish down, or a soft undercoat of feathers. As the chicks grow, their other feathers begin to develop under the down.

parents vomit up food they ate earlier for the young to eat. Adult vultures maintain long-term relationships with each other too. Most of the birds in a roost are relatives, but sometimes unrelated birds form bonds. Groups of vultures sometimes work together to drive their rivals away from a roost. Relatives, friends, and mates groom each other. Preening keeps black vultures' feathers clean and smooth. Well-maintained feathers help the birds fly and stay warm.

Roosting together helps black vultures find meals. If some vultures fed on a big carcass the day before, other vultures follow them back to the carcass in the morning. Black vultures also form foraging groups. A group has more eyes watching the ground, so it has a greater chance of finding something tasty than one bird alone does. Black vultures spy on other scavengers too. Most birds, including black vultures, have a poor sense of smell. But turkey vultures do not. Turkey vultures can sniff out a dead animal even when leaves cover the carcass. Black vultures will follow a turkey vulture that appears to have smelled something good.

When they find a carcass, many black vultures gather to feed on it. Sometimes one group of related vultures fights with another group. The larger group takes control of the food. Vultures also use their numbers to fight other scavengers. A single black

VULTURES IN TROUBLE

Vultures perform an important job by cleaning up dead animals. Dead animals can carry harmful diseases. When vultures eat dead animals, they not only remove waste from the land but also help control the spread of diseases. However, many vulture species are in trouble. People kill the birds for food and other products. They also poison vultures both on purpose and by accident. In the 1990s, many farmers in India used a drug called diclofenac to treat their cows. Diclofenac killed vultures that fed on dead cows. The drug was banned in 2006. But scientists estimate that between 2000 and 2005, the falling vulture population led to more than 100,000 human deaths a year from disease.

vulture might not be able to defeat a turkey vulture. But a group of black vultures can chase the other species away. Another scavenger that lives in the Americas is the Andean condor. Its wingspan measures up to 10.5 feet (3 m), broader than any other raptor in the world. By banding together, black vultures can keep Andean condors away from a carcass.

Black vultures hunt live prey very rarely. But they sometimes

Black vultures sometimes fight each other to claim food or to protect feeding areas. They may fight by spreading their wings, biting, or pecking.

go after small or young animals. A group of vultures might surround the prey. Then they attack it together. This is another way that black vultures find strength in numbers.

CHAPTER FOUR

AMERICAN CROWS

American crows are large, social, and smart. These black birds are about 17 to 21 inches (43 to 53 cm) long. Crow families spend time together all year round, and winter roosts can include as many as two million birds. American crows and their relatives have big brains, which they use to communicate, work together, and learn from each other.

During the breeding season, American crows live throughout the United States

American crows roost and build nests in large trees. Some flocks gather near landfills, dumpsters, or other man-made structures.

HELPFUL WOODPECKERS

Like crows, acorn woodpecker parents have helpers. This bird's range stretches from the western United States to northern South America. The birds work together to store thousands of acorns in trees as a food source. Groups can consist of parents and helpers. Sometimes as many as four mothers lay eggs in the same nest. Their offspring might stay in the group for as long as five years while helping their younger relatives. Scientists have found that larger groups of acorn woodpeckers can raise more chicks than a single woodpecker can.

and Canada. They spend the winter mostly in the southern half of their range. Crows are omnivores. They eat almost anything they can manage to find. Their diet includes insects, small animals, eggs, plants, carrion, and human leftovers.

American crows live in various habitats. The species thrives around humans. In the past, people associated crows with death partly because of their role as scavengers. A group of crows is even called a murder.

Crow helpers may gather materials such as twigs or grasses to use for building nests. They also feed chicks by throwing up food into their mouths.

FAMILY LIFE

American crows are family birds. A family might consist of only a mated pair. Other times, the pair has helpers. These helpers are often young crows. They are sometimes but not always related to the mated pair. Some helpers are grown-up offspring of the pair. Families share and defend a territory, although they

American crows sometimes defend their roosting sites by chasing or attacking larger birds such as hawks or eagles.

may forage elsewhere during the day or go to a roost at night. Families also raise young together. Crow helpers assist with building nests or caring for eggs. Some helpers bring food to the mother or her chicks.

By cooperating, a large family can raise more chicks than a smaller family. Helpers benefit too. Parents often provide food for helpers, even though they're not chicks anymore. Helpers also get to stay in their home territory for a longer time. They can spend time learning and growing before starting their own families.

LIFE IN A MURDER

American crows often spend the night in roosts. Doing so helps them stay safe and find food. Crow flocks also provide protection during the day. When a crow spies a predator, it loudly scolds the animal. The scolding is a signal to attract other crows. The crows work together to drive the predator away. By watching each other

A MEMORY FOR FACES

Scientists have discovered that crows can remember human faces. They noticed that crows react to individual people. If the crows think a person is scary, they often mob or scold the person. Crows also seek out people who have given them food in the past. In 2006, scientists wanted to find out how American crows recognized humans. Researchers wore masks with different faces, including a scary Halloween mask, while catching the crows. Later, the crows pestered whoever was wearing the scary mask. The crows also taught other crows to fear the face. Years later, crows that hatched after the experiment still scolded the scary mask.

American crows use their sharp beaks and talons to hold, pick up, and tear into food such as fish.

and responding to scolding calls, crows can learn when dangerous animals are near.

Crows also work as a group to steal food from other species. Some crows might catch the attention of an animal that has food while another crow swoops in to steal the food. Sometimes crows call to each other when gathering around a large food source. These calls invite other crows to feed. This gathering gives crows a chance to get to know each other too. They can see who is dominant or meet a potential mate.

STRAIGHT TO THE SOURCE

Scientist John Marzluff and naturalist Tony Angell wrote a book about crow intelligence. In it, they discuss how crows might understand what other creatures are thinking. They tell a story about a woman who saw crows outsmarting geese in British Columbia, Canada:

> *[Valerie Allmendinger] noticed [a] cook tossing whole slices of bread to a small flock of Canada geese. But the geese got none of the bread. Instead, a dozen crows assembled and quickly concealed [the bread] from the geese. For twenty minutes, each bird picked up a large, red maple leaf and placed it exactly on top of a bread slice. As the geese headed toward the bread, they seemed confused at its rapid disappearance. Under these circumstances the hungry geese did not understand that the bread was still right in front of them, just under the leaves.*

Source: John Marzluff and Tony Angell. *Gifts of the Crow.* Free Press, 2012.

WHAT'S THE BIG IDEA?

Take a close look at this passage. What is the main connection being made between crow behavior and crow intelligence? What can you tell about how crows understand other animals according to this excerpt?

CHAPTER FIVE

CHINSTRAP PENGUINS

Chinstrap penguins stand about 28 inches (71 cm) tall and can live up to 20 years. With a population of around eight million, chinstrap penguins are one of the most numerous penguin species in the world. They also form some of the largest nesting colonies, or rookeries. Around 375 colonies are spread across the Antarctic coastline and nearby islands. One colony on Zavodovski Island includes more than a million adult chinstrap penguins. During the winter,

Large chinstrap penguin colonies can be found on islands near Antarctica, including the South Orkney Islands and the South Shetland Islands.

the ocean around Antarctica freezes. The penguins move north to find open water.

Chinstrap penguins need open water to forage for krill, a food source that makes up most of the species' diet. Krill are related to shrimp and crabs. Although each krill is only about 2.4 inches (6 cm) long, huge krill populations live in the Antarctic Ocean.

COUNTING PENGUINS

Counting chinstrap penguins isn't easy. Scientists do this to keep track of the population. Since the penguins nest on remote islands, it's difficult to get to their colonies. Scientists must sail on rough seas and make difficult landings. At a colony, some nests are on steep slopes that are hard to climb. Scientists use several methods to count penguins in a colony. In some places, scientists count in person. In others, scientists take photos of the colony from above. They may take pictures with drones, or flying robots. They use the photos to estimate population numbers. Other pictures are taken from space.

NESTING IN NUMBERS

Like most other penguin species, chinstrap penguins

ANTARCTIC FOOD WEB

A food web is a network of food chains in an ecosystem. This food web shows food chains in the Antarctic. What do you notice about how chinstrap penguins are linked to other species on the food web? How does the web help you better understand Chapter Five of this book?

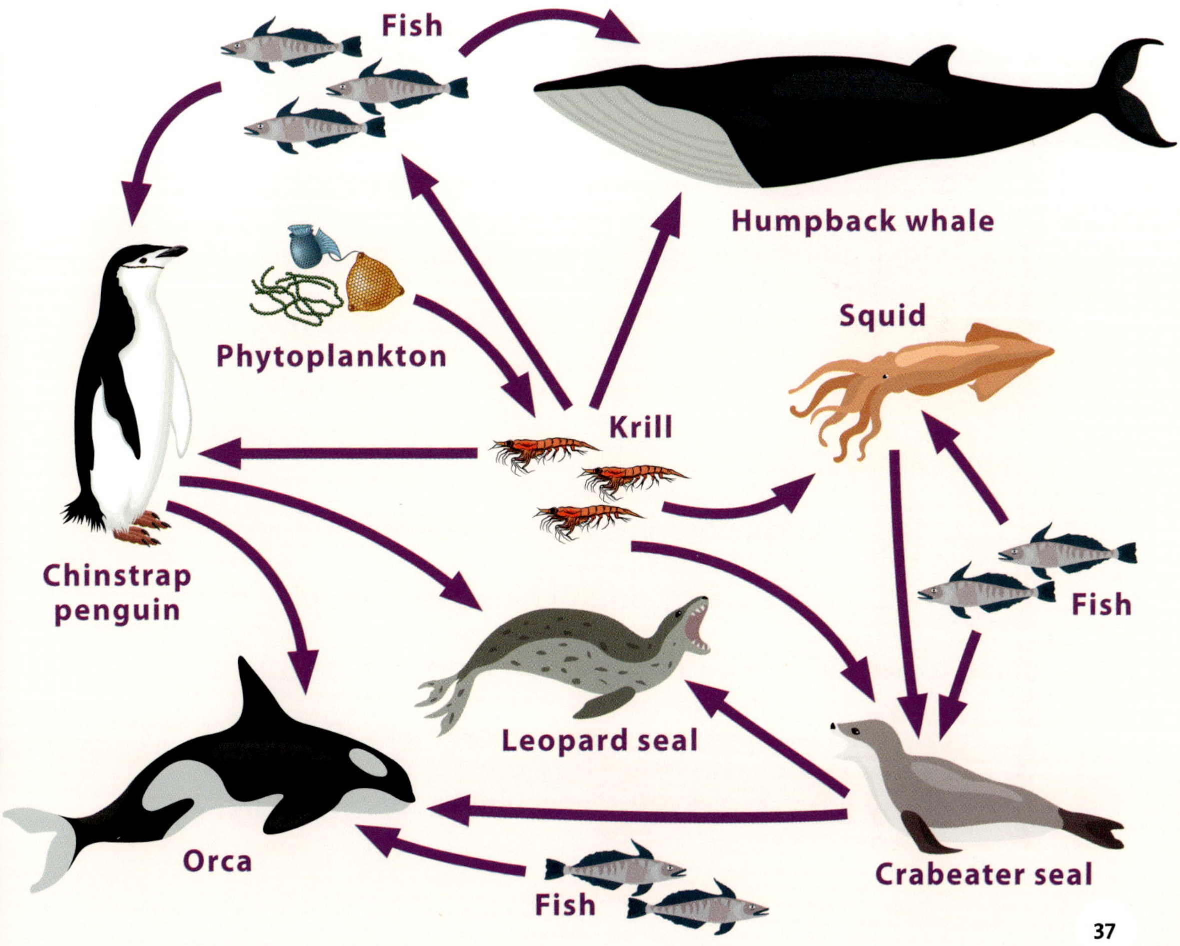

Chinstrap penguins lay two eggs at a time, and parents take turns sitting on the eggs to keep them warm. After hatching, chicks stay in the nest for about a month.

nest on land. They often nest beside two other species, Adélie penguins and gentoo penguins. The penguins arrive at their colonies during the Antarctic spring. They build nests by scraping the ground and then making a pile of stones.

Living in large colonies helps protect penguins from predators. Healthy adult chinstrap penguins don't have to worry about predators on land, but seabirds such as skuas eat penguin eggs and chicks. Penguins in a colony also shield eggs and chicks from deadly

Antarctic weather. Even during summer, the Antarctic is cold and windy. Nests in the center of a group are warmer and more protected than nests near the edges. More eggs hatch in the center of the group. These eggs hatch faster than others too.

GROWING IN GROUPS

Krill live in the ocean, so chinstrap penguin parents must leave the colony to forage. At first, one parent stays at the nest to protect the offspring. When chicks get older, both parents leave at the same time. To stay safe and warm,

BABY FLOCKS

Penguins aren't the only birds whose youngsters form groups. Crèches also occur in the nesting colonies of many other seabirds and waterbirds. While penguin chicks in a crèche are on their own, that's not true for other species. For example, flamingo adults and birds below the breeding age watch over flamingo crèches. Ostriches also end up with large flocks of chicks. Sometimes two ostrich families fight, and the winning side takes all the babies. After a few battles, an adult ostrich couple can end up caring for 300 chicks.

Young chinstrap penguins join crèches after staying in the nest for 20 to 30 days. Many other types of penguins form these groups too.

chicks gather in groups called crèches. If a predator approaches, the group forms a tight pack to make it harder for the predator to single out one chick.

Crèches also protect chicks from unrelated adults. An adult penguin guarding a nest may attack a wandering chick. Adults also defend food meant for their own young.

When chinstrap penguin chicks are about two months old, they leave the colony and join other penguins at sea. After the long winter, the young birds return to the colony they grew up in. Like many other bird species, living in numbers helps them survive and thrive.

FURTHER EVIDENCE

Chapter Five talks about how chinstrap penguins live in groups. Identify one of the chapter's main points. What evidence does the author provide to support this point? Read the article at the website below. Does the information on the website support the main point of the chapter? Does it present new evidence?

CHINSTRAP PENGUINS

abdocorelibrary.com/bird-groups

FAST FACTS

- Some bird species live alone or in pairs. Others form large groups to stay safe, find food, or raise young.
- Red-billed queleas spend their lives in flocks. They eat, rest, and nest together. Some quelea flocks are made up of more than a million individuals.
- European starlings form roosts that contain more than a million birds, including other bird species.
- Starling flocks form murmurations. The quick movements made by murmurations help keep starlings safe from predators when they go to a roost for the night.
- Black vultures form groups to roost, forage, and feed.
- Black vultures work together to steal carcasses away from other scavengers.
- American crows live in family groups that raise offspring together. Parents have helpers who are often young crows from previous years. They help care for the family's offspring.
- Crows work together to chase off predators. Crows also communicate and warn each other about dangerous animals.

- Chinstrap penguins nest together in colonies called rookeries. These can include more than a million adult birds.
- Chinstrap penguin chicks gather in crèches when they get older. The crèches protect chicks from predators and adult penguins.

STOP AND THINK

Surprise Me

Chapter Four discusses the social life of American crows. After reading this book, what two or three facts about American crows did you find most surprising? Write a few sentences about each fact. Why did you find each fact surprising?

Dig Deeper

After reading this book, what questions do you still have about how birds find strength in numbers? With an adult's help, find a few reliable sources that can help you answer your questions. Write a paragraph about what you learned.

Say What?

Studying bird behavior can mean learning a lot of new vocabulary. Find five words in this book you've never heard before. Use a dictionary to find out what they mean. Then write the meanings in your own words and use each word in a new sentence.

Another View

This book talks about black vultures. As you know, every source is different. Ask a librarian or another adult to help you find another source about black vultures. Write a short essay comparing and contrasting the new source's point of view with that of this book's author. What is the point of view of each author? How are they similar and why? How are they different and why?

GLOSSARY

carcass
the body of a dead animal

endothermic
describing an animal that can make its own body heat and maintain its body temperature

forage
to search for food

habitat
a place where an animal normally lives

migrate
to move from one place or region to another

omnivore
an animal that eats both plants and other animals

raptor
a bird of prey, such as a hawk, owl, or vulture

roost
a place where birds gather to rest or sleep; also, to gather together to rest or sleep

scavenger
an animal that eats animals that are already dead

species
a group of animals that can mate and have offspring with each other

vertebrate
an animal with a backbone or spine

ONLINE RESOURCES

To learn more about bird groups, visit our free resource websites below.

Core Library CONNECTION
FREE! COMMON CORE MULTIMEDIA RESOURCES

Visit **abdocorelibrary.com** or scan this QR code for free Common Core resources for teachers and students, including vetted activities, multimedia, and booklinks, for deeper subject comprehension.

Booklinks NONFICTION NETWORK
FREE! ONLINE NONFICTION RESOURCES

Visit **abdobooklinks.com** or scan this QR code for free additional online weblinks for further learning. These links are routinely monitored and updated to provide the most current information available.

LEARN MORE

Debbink, Andrea. *Birds of Prey*. Abdo, 2023.

Hoare, Ben. *An Anthology of Exquisite Birds*. DK, 2024.

Mayntz, Melissa. *Birds for Kids*. Sourcebooks, 2024.

INDEX

About the Author

Clara MacCarald is a freelance writer with a master's degree in ecology and natural resources. She lives with her family in an off-grid house in the forests of central New York and writes nonfiction books for children.